NO LONGER PROPERTY OF
ANYTHINK LIBRARIES/
RANGEVIEW LIBRARY DISTRICT

D0772263

My culture

Bobbie Kalman

 Crabtree Publishing Company

www.crabtreebooks.com

Created by Bobbie Kalman

Author and Editor-in-Chief
Bobbie Kalman

Reading consultant
Elaine Hurst

Editors
Kathy Middleton
Crystal Sikkens

Photo research
Bobbie Kalman

Design
Bobbie Kalman
Katherine Berti

Production coordinator and Prepress technician
Katherine Berti

Illustrations
Barbara Bedell: page 17

Photographs by Shutterstock

Library and Archives Canada Cataloguing in Publication

Kalman, Bobbie, 1947-
   My culture / Bobbie Kalman.

(My world)
Includes index.
ISBN 978-0-7787-9518-6 (bound).--ISBN 978-0-7787-9543-8 (pbk.)

   1. Culture--Juvenile literature. I. Title. II. Series: My world
(St. Catharines, Ont.)

GN357.K33 2011   j306   C2010-901978-4

Library of Congress Cataloging-in-Publication Data

Kalman, Bobbie.
  My culture / Bobbie Kalman.
    p. cm. -- (My world)
  Includes index.
  ISBN 978-0-7787-9543-8 (pbk. : alk. paper) -- ISBN 978-0-7787-9518-6
(reinforced library binding : alk. paper)
  1. Culture--Juvenile literature. I. Title. II. Series.

  GN357.K35 2010
  306--dc22
                   2010011305

Crabtree Publishing Company

www.crabtreebooks.com   1-800-387-7650

Printed in China/072010/AP20100226

Copyright © **2011 CRABTREE PUBLISHING COMPANY**. All rights reserved. No part of this publication may be reproduced, stored in a retrieval system or be transmitted in any form or by any means, electronic, mechanical, photocopying, recording, or otherwise, without the prior written permission of Crabtree Publishing Company. In Canada: We acknowledge the financial support of the Government of Canada through the Book Publishing Industry Development Program (BPIDP) for our publishing activities.

Published in Canada
Crabtree Publishing
616 Welland Ave.
St. Catharines, Ontario
L2M 5V6

Published in the United States
Crabtree Publishing
PMB 59051
350 Fifth Avenue, 59th Floor
New York, New York 10118

Published in the United Kingdom
Crabtree Publishing
Maritime House
Basin Road North, Hove
BN41 1WR

Published in Australia
Crabtree Publishing
386 Mt. Alexander Rd.
Ascot Vale (Melbourne)
VIC 3032

What is in this book?

What is culture?

Culture is the way we live.
It is the clothes we wear
and the foods we eat.
Culture is how we have fun.
Culture is always changing.

People live in 195 **countries**.
The people in different countries
have different cultures.
What is the name of your country?

Find your country
on a map or globe.

Saying hello

Part of my culture is the **language** I speak.

I speak English.

I am learning to say hello
in some other languages.

Can you say hello in these languages?

Say hello!

Hola (Spanish)

Bonjour (French)

Guten Tag (German)

Nǐ hǎo (Chinese)

Konnichiwa (Japanese)

Do your parents speak
more than one language?
Which languages can you speak?

Special clothes

The clothes I wear are part of my Indonesian culture.
My friends and I wear shirts like these.
We wear caps on our heads.

On special days,
I wear the clothes
of my Russian culture.
I wear these clothes
when I dance.

Yummy foods!

Food is part of culture.
I like tasting foods
from different countries.
Which of these foods
have you tasted?

pizza (Italy)

sushi
(Japan)

chips and salsa
(Mexico)

salad (Greece)

curry (India)

Have you ever eaten with **chopsticks**?

Playing sports

Sports are part of my culture.

I play soccer, football, and baseball.

I like to play basketball, too.

soccer

basketball

baseball

football

12

skateboarding

skiing

Are you a
skateboarder?
Do you ski?
Which is your
favorite sport?

Music and dance

Music and dancing are part of culture. My friend and I play different **musical instruments**. We like to play music from our cultures.

hulusi
(Chinese)

accordion
(Polish)

Dancing is a fun part
of my culture.
I wear this dress when
I do Spanish dancing.

Special holidays

My family spends **holidays** together.
We eat turkey dinners on Thanksgiving
and on Christmas Day.

Before Christmas,
we decorate a tree.
Santa Claus brings gifts
on Christmas Eve.
We spend Christmas
Day with our family.

Celebrating culture

To **celebrate** is to have fun.
Which of these special days
do you celebrate?
How do you celebrate them?

Cinco de Mayo

Diwali

birthday   Eid   Halloween

Mother's Day

Easter

Hanukkah

Valentine's
Day

St. Patrick's
Day

Father's Day

19

The art of culture

People show their cultures through art.

Art is a way we show our imagination.

All the things you see here are art.

This building is art.

It is called the Taj Mahal.

This fan is art.

This picture is art.

This doll is art.

My costume
and dance
are art.

21

Fun with culture

There are many cultures in our country.
Learning about other cultures is fun.
Which part of culture do you like best?

Do you
like
holidays?

Do you
like
food?

Do you like
music?

Do you like
sports?

Words to know and Index

art
pages 20–21

clothes
pages
4, 8–9

countries
pages 5, 22

foods
pages 4, 10–11, 22

fun
pages
4, 15,
18, 22

holidays
(celebrations)
pages
16–19, 22

languages
pages 6–7

music (dance)
pages 9, 14–15,
21, 22

sports
pages 12–13, 22

Notes for adults

Objectives
- to introduce children to the different ways of life of people
- to show ways in which language, stories, clothing, food, sports, holidays, music, and dance influence the ways people behave and express themselves
- to allow children to share their heritage and learn about the cultures of other children in the class

Read along
Ask the children to read *My culture* along with you. Do any of them speak a language shown on page 6?
Could they say hello in that language? Have the children practice saying the five hello greetings by repeating them after you say them.
Have them walk around the room saying hello to one another in these different languages.
As you read the book together, focus attention on the different ways people dress, the foods they eat, the sports they play, the music they play or dance to, and the special ways they celebrate.

Class discussion
Ask the children which foods on pages 10–11 they like to eat and point out the countries of origin of those foods on a wall map.

Activity: Hands around the world
Have each of the children make a cutout of one hand, on which they will print their name. Tape the hands around a large map and link each hand, using colored yarn, to the country or culture of each child.

Extensions
Ask the children to make flags from the countries of their origins. Have them print their names on the flags and display the flags on a bulletin board.

Share the *What is culture?* book with the class. This book shows in detail the different aspects of culture.

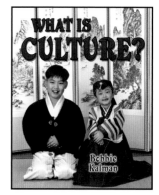

From ***Our Multicultural World*** series
Guided Reading: P

For teacher's guide, go to www.crabtreebooks.com/teachersguides